I0014523

Google SEO Advanced 2.0

"The Ultimate Web Development & Search Engine Optimization Guide for Webmasters"

By: **Ryan Wade Brown**

This publication is intended to provide latest, accurate, authoritative, useful, practical, user friendly and updated details regarding the topic covered. It is supplied in the earnest understanding that the author and publisher is not engaged in any promotion, marketing or any other activities connected with any Google or search marketing related business or industry.

For the safety of your business, you are suggested to read and understand the principles given in this book, before applying any of the tips or suggestions to your business. This book is sold to the readers for the purpose of information and knowledge.

The author or the web site does not accept any risk or responsibilities arising out of using the techniques or methods mentioned in the book, nor do they are responsible for any loss or damages that result from actions or decisions made/taken by the purchasers of the book.

The author has taken enough and reasonable care to assure that the information, details and tips given in this book are as accurate as possible. However, the buyer of this book may realize that search marketing and SEO (Search Engine Optimization) is an ever-changing and dynamic industry, where the information available keeps changing almost everyday.

Thus, the information provided does not constitute legal or professional marketing advice of any type or kind. This product is sold to you under **NO Liability clause** and the product comes to you in an "**as is**" and "**without warranties**" condition. All trademarks, trade names, services marks and logos referenced herein belong to their respective companies.

Thanks a lot for purchasing this book! I am Ryan Wade Brown and I am the owner of a website called www. RyanWadeBrown.com. I am glad that you made an intelligent and important decision to purchase, read, and learn hitherto unknown and insider secrets about Google SEO techniques.

There are several reasons and considerations, why I complied and wrote this book for you. Available books available in the market on Google SEO and its amazing principles are too complicated and complex to read and understand.

Google SEO is a profitable and viable technology that can provide a stable platform to launch your business by attaining higher search engine rankings. However, it is also complicated as well, especially for a newbie entrepreneur.

The main objective of writing this book is to provide you an updated and complete manual that provides you all the necessary information and details to kick start your campaign.

Being a sensitive subject, Google SEO need proper understanding and study, which I believe will become easier and uncomplicated with this practical and hands-on manual. I know that there are hundreds of good books, reports and magazines on this dicey topic. I still believe that most of them are good and contain useful information.

However, what I found with them was that they were filled with too many pages of difficult to read and hard to understand details and information. The book you are reading now will give you unbiased and most relevant information (I really hope and believe!) on a highly lucrative ad-marketing concept called Google SEO.

With this book, you can learn and understand more about this exciting topic and later use the basic principles to launch your SEO campaign in a big way. I am also glad ad happy to say that this book contains a number of useful, beneficial and practical tips and suggestions that will empower and guarantee you to host your Google SEO campaign with unlimited success.

I can really vouch and attest for the authenticity and practical usefulness of this little manual and the benefits that it can provide you and to your business.

Contents

What is Search Engine Optimization?

Search engine optimization is an intricate art of making your web site secure very high position in Google search engine. When internet users query a search engine like Google with preferred keywords, it will return with a long list of web sites within the shortest possible time.

However, the results that appear on the first few pages of the search result are the most successful and relevant results for an internet user. The Google search engine index is very vast and voluminous, and it has the marvelous ability to return the most relevant search results.

An internet user who uses Google engine will never browse beyond the second page of the search results. If Google does not list your web site on top two or three pages of the search engine, it may never be visible to the internet user. The process of making your web site appear in the topmost pages of Google search engine is a lengthy and critical operation. It is also time consuming and manual in nature.

Tip: Search engine optimization is a technique that has an uncanny ability to communicate effectively with the Google search engine. Google search engine knows exactly how your web site is constructed and in what manner you tweak your web pages for optimization. SEO is more about securing a very high level of search engine presence, by using a number of well-optimized keywords and phrases linked closely with your business theme.

Benefits of SEO

SEO gives you a number of significant benefits and strategic advantages over other non-optimized web sites. Here are some of those advantages:

1. SEO can influence the way in which a site visitor looks and feels about your web site.

2. You can create a brand identity for your web site.

3. People can easily recall your business theme and brand.

4. You can increase the targeted traffic and inbound links to your web site

5. It is very easy to position and maneuver web site pages.

6. You can even dominate and strengthen your business, by using a number of mirror sites.

7. SEO can yield a very good rate of return (ROI) over your investment.

8. It is also possible to boost the sales of products and services.

9. The cost acquiring and retaining potential customers will be quite low, when you use a good SEO technique.

10. You can enhance your web presence by increasing your product's market share.

11. It is very easy to compete with large players on the web. SEO implementation makes your web site visible and available throughout the year.

13. SEO is perhaps the best tool available for web site promotion and advertisement.

14. It is also the cheapest marketing promotion tool available on the internet.

What Is a Search Engine?

All internet users know and understand how search engines work and in what manner they provide us the search results. The procedure is quite simple – just type a word into the search box and hit the *Go* button to generate a long list of web sites and links.

Nevertheless, most of us do not know the intricate mechanism of indexing and retrieval and the manner in which it can extract all those web pages and their links. In fact, it is a sort of complicated and tedious operation.

Every search engine uses an efficient piece of software that employs a series of applications and processes, with an ability to extract sensitive information and details on thousands of web pages.

A typical search engine like Google works in the following manner:

1. The information and details collected is usually a series of keywords or phrases that indicate the type of content included in the web pages.

2. The keywords will also act as indicators of information included in the URL of the web page, divulge entire set of codes that make up the page, provide a series of links that establish connections to other web pages and any other sensitive details pertaining to the web site.

3. Once the search engine collects these bits of data, it will index and store them in an extensive database.

4. When a user searches for a specific keyword or term, the backend software uses an algorithm to inspect and evaluate the information already stored in the database.

4. Once the search engine accesses the index, the algorithm will start retrieving the links from the specific web pages that actually match the search term entered by the internet user.

Tip: An efficient virtual agent called spider or robot collects useful information on web pages of a web site.

These little utilities glance and crawl over every web page and collect necessary keywords or phrases on each of the web pages.

Google will then integrate this information into the database that acts as an efficient search engine for millions of web sites.

The innards of a search engine

There is much more to a search engine than just retrieving the necessary links from a web site! In fact, there are a number of smaller components attached to a search engine.

Query Interface: You will see this home page as soon as you type the URL of the search engine (Google). For example, the home page of www.google.com is the query interface for that search engine. There are many famous query interfaces known to internet users. However, Google offers the most comprehensive, user-interface that offers unlimited convenience to its users. Google's legendary ability put a web page on top of the search engine is all due to a web site's page optimization and page tweaking.

What are crawlers, spider and robots?

As soon as you log on to Google search engine, you will see the user interface with all its simple and easy to use features. Nevertheless, what hides behind that innocent looking interface is so vast and voluminous that you will ask yourself whether such a thing can really exist!

Spiders, crawlers or robots are those tiny utilities that crawl and zoom around the web pages to catalogue or index the available data and information from millions of web sites.

What is database?

A typical Google database is a large and voluminous storage area that holds thousands of data points on each URL existing on the web. Google ranks and indexes individual databases in a number of ways, whereas the method of ranking or retrieval of data is specific to each search engine.

What is a search algorithm?

Search algorithm is an important unit that acts as an efficient cog in the wheel. The manner in which a search engine works depends on the nature of the algorithm or the manner in which the user discovers the data or information.

Tip: A search algorithm works in its own unique manner! It employs a series of procedures to work in the following manner:

- ✓ *Analyzes the existing problem to find out most possible solutions*
- ✓ *It can sweep the entire database that holds important keywords and URLs related to those keywords.*
- ✓ *Retrieve thousands of web pages that contain words or phrases searched by the site visitor.*
- ✓ *Conduct a search operation located either in the body of the web page or in a URL that actually links to the page.*

Fact: Each search engine is unique and special, as the search algorithm used by every search engine is different and special.

Some common types of search algorithms are:

List Search: A special algorithm, it conducts an exhaustive search through the available database while looking for a single search key. The type of search is linear, while the method used is list style. When you conduct this type of search, the result could be a small list of data retrieved out of a big database of millions of web pages.

Tree Search: This search depends on retrieving the data from the broadest possible to the most narrow or from the narrowest to the broadest data sets that are similar to a branched tree, where the data set can branch and spread over to a number of sub branches. Tree search is a very useful method of search.

SQL Search: This search is non-hierarchical in nature and you can search the web by using any sub set data.

Informed Search: This search provides a specific answer to a specific set of questions of queries.

About retrieval and ranking: Retrieval of data in the form of web pages is the most important aspect of a search engine. This intricate process is a subtle combination of three critical components – crawler, the database and search algorithm. All these three components work in tandem to cull out the words or phrase that you use on the search engine. However, the trickiest part of the entire operation is the ranking procedure performed by the search engine.

Tip: Ranking in a search engine = A measure of how many times net users see a particular web page.

However, in the manner a search engine works to assign a rank to a web site is matter of confidentiality and secrecy. *SEO is an intricate process of tweaking a web site to reach the top of the search engine.* Different search engines use different types of ranking methodologies. Google search engine considers a number of ranking criteria while assigning ranks to a web site:

Location: Location means the area that houses keywords and phrases on a web page.

For example, let us say that you are searching for some information based on a keyword called "fresh flowers". Most of the search engines will assign ranks to the available results according to the area occupied on the page, where the keyword actually appears.

In some cases, the web page in question may be having a higher rank depending on the number of keywords used in the web site. If you include the keyword in the title tag of the web page, your web site may appear on top of the search page. It means that a web site designed without applying the basic techniques of SEO may appear far behind in the search pages.

Frequency: The rate or frequency at which the searched term appears on a given web page will also influence the ranking and indexing on the web pages

For example, let us assume that a person X uses the keyword fresh flowers almost eight times in the web page, while another person Y uses it only four times. Now, it is obvious that the web pages belonging to person X appears on top of the search pages.

This is in comparison to the page owned by the person "Y". Google does not like keyword spamming and you may not use too many keywords stuffed within a single page.

Links: A web page with lots of incoming and outgoing links will appear on top of the search engine, when compared to another page that lacks such links. Links that go out of the sites, links that come into the site and the number of links within a web site are all quite important for the success of SEO. Furthermore, the links supplied must be accurate enough to get a top ranking.

Click-through: The total number of click-through that your site receives could be an important indictor of ranking criteria. Some search engines monitor the total number of clicks that a particular web site receives, before assigning ranking to the web site.

The future ranking may also depend on the previous history of the web site in relation to its click-through rates. Page raking is a very precise and cumbersome process, while the process of assigning ranking to web sites depends on the techniques and methods used by Google search engine.

You may need to use one or more of the techniques given above to push your web site on to the topmost pages of the search engines.

Classification of search engines: All search engines are different and each one of them works differently with its own search mechanism and technology.

There are three major types of search engines:

Primary search engines: A majority of search engines belongs to this category and they help you generate a considerable amount of traffic to your web site. In fact, these search engines help you reach top of the search pages by using efficient SEO techniques.

Google is perhaps the most widely used search engine in the web world and it is the undisputed king of the lot. It is accurate, easy to use, efficient and very quick. Link popularity of a web site and its keywords are two of the most critical factors that Google considers before assigning page ranking to a web site.

Secondary search engines: Google always targets specialized and specific audiences, who need specific and precise search results. Google does not provide any traffic or inbound links to your web site, but provide specialized and accurate search results. Some examples are Lycos and Ask.com.

Google search engine works and assigns ranks based on the reciprocal links and keywords, while a number of other search engines consider the Meta tags as an important criterion for ranking purposes.

Targeted search engines: These are the topical search engines, because they are the most specific and accurate search engines of all. These are very narrow, highly specific, and usually attributed to a general topic. Some examples are City Search, Yahoo Travels, and Political Information etc.

SEO Fundamentals

Search engine optimization is the art and science of creating a web portal that appears very high up in search engine pages. In other words, you will be maximizing your site's ability to secure top search engine rankings.

It also means that any future course of actions that you take on your web site are intended to obtain or procure high ranking on Google.

Some of the basic elements of SEO are:

1. All entry and exit pages related to your website
2. Page titles of all web pages
3. Page content in all pages
4. General layout and architecture of web pages
5. Graphics and images embedded in the web site

However, these are only few of the required elements used for SEO. You may also consider a number of other elements for enabling SEO techniques. You may need to think of other elements like keyword density, links, HTML codes and Meta tags, while optimizing your web pages. Advertising and search marketing campaigns like Google AdWords, AdSense and affiliate programs are some other vital elements that make your web portal attain higher page rankings.

Tip: SEO is a delicate mixture of a number of elements that are specific to a web portal and its design and layout. SEO technology is a live and dynamic technology that keeps changing on a daily basis. It is also moving target that you need to monitor very carefully and later mentor on a consistent basis. SEO techniques keep changing as and when there is a new requirement imposed by the search engine.

How to tweak and manipulate search engines

Largely, SEO is all about manipulating the search engine to attain top search engine rankings. It could also be a surreptitious technique of pushing your web site on to the top of the search engine pages.

You can do a lot to manipulate a search engine like:

1. Design and construct a web portal that contains a number of Meta tags, interesting and keyword-enriched content, graphics and images and a series of targeted keywords that can eventually help your web portal reach top pages of a search engine.

2. Sprinkle a number of keywords liberally and in strategic places of an article, so that a search engine can crawl over them to extract your site and place it on top of the engine.

3. Set-up reciprocal links, so that search engines can consider them while assigning ranks.

4. Generate lot of web site traffic and inbound links to your web site, so that search engine can take these important bits of data into account before assigning rank.

5. Use manual submission method, to allow Google search engine recognize your site immediately.

However, you may also take note of a number of other negative parameters before using SEO methods to increase the ranking of your web site:

1. Hide a number of important keywords and phrases within the web pages to make your web site efficiently optimized for immediate Google search. This is a negative technique.

2. Artificial generation of links to your web portals from other sites, those are irrelevant to the theme of your web site.

3. Artificial generation of incoming traffic and links from sites those are irrelevant to the overall theme of your web site.

4. Repeated and automated site submission to force the web site to appear on the search pages.

5. Sending repeated mail to your search engine to include your site in the directory.

Tip: SEO is a slow and laborious process! You just cannot gate crash your way to reach the top of the search engine. You will need to use the best and legal methods to inch your way forward to reach the top. Take your time and the rank will come to you automatically.

Designing SEO Blueprint

Before optimizing your web portal for Google search, you must have a solid and concrete SEO plan ready for immediate use. A concrete and well-designed SEO plan will help you know and understand, where you can concentrate your efforts and how you can reduce the time required to optimize your site.

Though SEO techniques can keep changing from time to time, a solid, basic blueprint can assist you in maintaining the rhythm and tempo of the process. Nevertheless, you may need to keep changing your SEO techniques and strategies to make your site retain its top most position.

SEO Goals

Webmasters must learn and understand why the need SEO in the first place. What are the benefits of using SEO? What should be your top goals for SEO? A failed SEO attempt is the perceived lack of clearly defined and well designed SEO technique built and nurtured around your immediate business needs and requirements.

Thus, you should set and act on a well-defined set of goals that eventually helps you reach the desired page ranks on Google search.

Some of the important objectives or goals of setting up a formidable SEO plan are:

1. Increase page ranks on Google

2. Advertise your web site to the entire web world

3. Increase online business revenue and enhance profits

4. Help assist the site to gain lot of traffic

5. Generate incoming and outgoing links

How to create a SEO plan

The most important objective or goal of creating a SEO plan is to help you stay on course, while working on the right type of SEO strategies and techniques. Creating a SEO plan is very frustrating and strenuous. It is also a very slow and painstaking process.

Here are some simple techniques that help you create a SEO plan:

Prioritizing web pages: You should look at your web site as individual chunks or pieces. Just take a deep look at each page of your web site and make a solid plan to promote each one of them.

Act on your top priorities to pick the most important pages that need immediate optimization and tweaking. Once you plan your initial technique, you can repeat the same technique on other web pages.

In fact, your site visitors may like to visit the most important page first before checking the other pages. The home page is obviously the first page that a site visitor would like to see first before navigating to other pages.

By applying the right type of SEO technique, you can also create a blueprint for your advanced marketing techniques. SEO and marketing actually go hand in hand and in close partnership. You may need to create and design a comprehensive and complete SEO plan that is suitable for your web site.

Evaluation of web site: Once you set and establish your priorities and goals, the next immediate step will be assessing and evaluating your web site to learn and understand:

1. Where exactly are you are standing right now
2. Where do you want to be in future
3. In what manner you want to use the SEO technique with changing scenarios.

Tip: One of the most important tips is to assess and evaluate your site on a page-by-page basis than web site as a whole.

SEO is a technology that should focus on all individual pages rather than the whole site.

You should concentrate and focus on enhancing each individual page to make your site SEO-enabled for achieving higher rankings. You may also need to consider a number of critical elements and attributes while conducting an evaluation:

Tagging: Meta tags are quite essential to list your site properly on a search engine.

Title tags and description tags are very important as well, while you are optimizing your site.

Page content: The quality and relevancy of content that you publish in your site is very critical for SEO success. People have the habit of looking for good and meaningful content that can provide them knowledgeable and practical information.

Keyword enriched content is the soul of a web site, and search engines simply love and adore properly written content inserted with the right type of keywords.

Links: Site links (incoming and outgoing) are very critical to the ultimate success of SEO campaign. Search engine crawlers and spiders demand active and live links in your web site, so that they can collect enough data and information about your site.

However, the links that you provide must be specific and special to your site and they should be relevant to the business theme as well. Broken links are dangerous for your SEO campaign.

Site map: Site map is an essential component of a web site. It is a XML document listed in the root of your HTML folder. Site map provides updated information and details like URLs, title of individual pages, relevance of pages and other vital information listed within the web site. Site map is also a good index of your web site.

Once you lay a solid foundation, the next immediate need is to list all those areas, which need instant correction and modifications. Simple and minor changes to some pages, or a tweak or two to another, will make your site suitably optimized for better performance. The overall picture must be simple and straightforward, so that you know and understand vital steps to make your web site SEO compliant.

What is organic SEO?

Some people use simple and plain SEO techniques to optimize their web sites. Organic SEO techniques are almost similar to other techniques, except that you are not using any advanced and new technologies, or spend more time on page optimization.

Organic SEO techniques ensure that all natural elements of SEO come to active play during page optimization, by developing on each of these elements to create a web portal that will one day appear on top of the major search engine pages.

Organic SEO technique may need more than a year to show the desired results.

Enabling Organic SEO

Enabling organic SEO can take a long time! It also needs the right type of elements and exact targeting of your web pages. Even with all hard work, you can still find that your site appearing somewhere on the tenth page of search results. However, judicious use of different elements and attributes can result in better SEO and very good page ranks.

The first right step that you can employ here is to ensure that you are optimizing all organic elements of the web portal to the best of their abilities.

Some of these basic elements are:

Content: Keyword stuffing is an undesirable act (also known as black-hat technique). In fact, Google does not like keyword stuffing. Keyword stuffing is an artificial method that tries to improve or enhance search engine ranking.

Good web site content is the most important aspect of SEO technology. The content that you publish on your site is very critical to the commercial success of your web site. Content could be anything; you can publish articles, snippets, blog columns, product descriptions and whitepapers those can make your site content-rich.

Spiders and crawlers have a tendency to crawl and search through the entire content to search for very relevant keywords and phrases. However, content alone is not enough to make your site SEO enabled; you will also need to match the keywords with Meta Tags and links.

You may also pay attention to update and edit the content to keep ahead to match the pace of Google's search spiders and crawlers.

Keywords: Keywords are the essential and mandatory parts of your web site and you will need to choose the best possible keywords that are relevant to the theme of your web site.

In essence, selection of right kind of keywords is a tricky art, and you will need to learn how to master the skill of selecting or choosing the best possible keywords for your web site.

In fact, you must focus your time and energy to see what exactly your customers are searching for on Google search. Let us say that you are searching for some products related to fresh flowers.

Let us assume that you have chosen a special keyword "fresh flowers" for this purpose. However, this keyword may be too vague and inadequate for making a specific search on Google.

The needs and requirements of an internet user may vary substantially, as people tend to look for a specific product or service, while they are conducting a search operation on Google.

To optimize your web pages, ensure that you are choosing more specific, niche and special keywords related to fresh flowers.

Google Analytics is one of the best web application utility that helps you track the web site traffic. Find it at the web page:

http://www.google.com/analytics.

What you need to do: Just copy a small piece of text block into the coding page of your web site. Once you insert the code, Google will take some time to accumulate vital information and forward it to your web site. In time, you will also get a detailed report about your site and its real progress.

With real time data gathering and accumulation, you will have an access to most commonly used keywords and phrases used by internet surfers. You can even combine the goodness of Google Analytics with Google AdWords to derive the best possible advantage in terms of SEO.

Internal and external links: Out-going and incoming links are vital to your SEO campaign.

How and where the links go or come in, are also very critical to your successful SEO campaign. Links could be internal, incoming or even outgoing; the more the number of these links, the better will be your chances to enhance the search engine ranking of your web site.

Broken and irrelevant links are quite bad for SEO practice. Ensure that the links that you provide through your web site are organic, related and relevant. Too many links within your web site may create a condition known as link farming and this is dangerous to your SEO as well.

Ensure that you are creating links that are highly specific and relevant to your web pages. Avoid all those links that are irrelevant to your SEO objectives.

Internal links are also very essential for a well-optimized web site. Internal links can take you from one page to the other and Google spider will take a deep look at your pages to assess the relevancy of the site for search engine ranking. A site map is a useful tool to enhance the image of your web site.

In what manner you create that site map is also critical; you can provide a simple page with very few links or you can chose to create a comprehensive page containing all the links in the web site. However, even a simple site map page can be too overpowering, if your site has too many web pages.

Web site user experience: This is actually very difficult to quantify, as each user is different in his or her taste and preferences. Nevertheless, user experience will be satisfactory, when an internet user decides to come back many times to your site to check the content for products and services.

Today's search engines are highly advanced and technical in that they can effectively keep a track of results of pages visited by a user in the course of some time. It means that Google can keep an active track of all visitors who visit your web site.

Let us also consider this classical scenario. Let us assume here that an internet user is searching for some specific information on fresh flowers on Google search engine.

When he or she types the required keywords in the Google search bar, a series of pages will appear on the search page as an immediate response. In fact, users select a link based on what they read below the searched URL. In essence, most users click on the links listed in the first two or three search pages.

Here, you can arrive at a conclusion that most of the users get what they want in the first one or two search pages. However, Google also marks and indexes those sites that the users actually click on and navigate to the home page.

When many people click on the same link, the search algorithm mechanism embedded in the Google search engine considers the link as highly popular and thus places the link higher up in the page.

It is certainly possible for you to move your web site from its lower position by using a series of SEO techniques. Another type of user response is the *bounce.* A bounce occurs when a user decides to press the back button of the browser to jump back to the previous search page.

The rate or degree at which users decide to bounce from your web site is a clear indicator of the relevancy or usability of the site.

Tip: Ensure that you are using the right type of keywords to enhance the user experience, as well as the usability factors of the site.

Interactivity factors: Today's search engines provide a facility of interaction between the users and the web sites they are visiting. Search engine spiders always look for this particular factor when assigning ranking to the website.

The perceived factor of interaction between a web site and user could be anything - it could be a simple filling of form by an internet user or a downloading of a file or even sending an e-mail by using the contact-us form.

This likely interaction is very important, because when you influence your visitor to interact with your web site, you can make him or her satisfied user, who in turn may become deeply loyal to your site. This is converting a user into a goal or goal conversion.

The more frequently a site visitor comes to your site, the more likely it is that the person will help you elevate the search engine ranking of your web site. The factor of interactivity or interaction becomes very important, when you want to make your site SEO specific.

Goal conversion and customer satisfaction are the other two important factors that will help you create a solid SEO strategy.

In reality, organic SEO is very difficult to achieve and perform! The only way you can carry out this procedure is to create a systematic mode of plan for every web page, tweak it with relevant keywords, insert excellent content in strategic pages and later create a series of links with an ability to import lot of traffic to the site.

Different SEO Strategies

SEO is laborious and hard to achieve! It is time consuming! It is also very complex with a series of difficult techniques!

It also takes lot of time and efforts to optimize the right blend of components, so that search engines take a note of your web site and allot better ranking to the web site.

You are the master of your web portal and you are the designer of your SEO techniques. Right now, you do not have an access to an efficient or complete tool that can provide you all the necessary solutions to make your web site appear very high up in search pages.

The only solution is to create your own SEO blueprint and act on it to make your web site SEO compliant.

Though it looks very tedious and complex to you, SEO is very easy to work on and get desired results. Hard work and consistent application of different techniques will help you make your web site 100% SEO enabled.

Constructing a SEO site

Tip: SEO is a thoughtful and ingenious collection of well-designed strategies that will help you enhance the name of your web site.

The pace or speed at which Google indexes and ranks your web site depends on the efficiency of SEO technique used on your web pages.

SEO is a gradual and continuing process that occurs in a number of steps and stages. Well-calculated and calibrated application processes will help you reach your cherished goal. In many cases, you may find very tedious to decide which technique is better for you and your web site.

In some cases, a simple failure could be an invaluable lesson; in others, you may even hit a jackpot, when one of the simplest techniques will yield you the best possible result.

SEO is best done is a series of small steps and procedures! The manner and way in which you build your site is as crucial as any other issue.

Usually, a search engine spider and crawler will look for the number of links, tags and type of navigation before assigning ranks to the web site.

Tip: Consider implementing SEO before designing your web site. However, you will need more time and effort to make your web site pre-SEO enabled.

Learn about your target

Before designing a web site, you will need to identify the types of search engines you want to include in your planning. The overall objective is to get your web site indexed in most of the available search engines. There are three types of search engines:

Crawler based engines: Google uses an automated software program to make regular visits to the web site, read and index its contents. Once it carries out a detailed trip, it dispatches the collected information to a central repository. Indexing or indexed pages are two of the results that become useful in drawing out important search results, when a person conducts a search on Google.

Human enabled engines: This system relies on people submitting the information stored and organized in the index and retrieve it as search results.

Yahoo was a very good example of this system, when it created several directories to help internet users conduct a detailed search.

Hybrid type of search engines: It is a combination of web crawler and manual submission type of search technology. You can manually submit the site for indexing, while the indexing process is through a series of web crawler or spider. Most of today's search engines belong to this category.

Elements of web pages

Including properly attributed elements into your web site is very critical to SEO success. Proper indexing will ensure that your site includes all attributes and elements.

One of the most important elements of Google search engine is the relevancy of keywords inserted.

In fact, Google is a keyword centered search engine that responds very well to search queries based on carefully selected keywords. It also looks for site popularity and the number of inks in the web site.

Tags

Text is perhaps the most important component of a web site; in fact, keywords enriched content published on your web site is the most critical factor that a search engine like Google considers while indexing the web pages.

Keywords and phrases included in your web pages must match and synchronize the keywords used in the context, while the density of keywords inserted on the web pages can adversely affect the efficacy, efficiency of content published.

Tags

Two types of tags are essential for SEO technology. Meta tags and HTML tags are the two entities that can make your web pages appear higher up in the search engine pages.

Here is some basic information about these tags:

Meta Tags

Keyword tag	It appears where you mention the keywords relevant to the web site. Example: <meta name="keywords" content="SEO, search engine optimization, page rank">
Description tag	It gives a short description of the web page. Example: <meta name="description" content="The ultimate guide to choosing the best flowers!"

Tip: Note that only some search engines consider Meta tags as valid indicators of SEO. Thus, you may need to use both Meta tags and HTML tags in your web site to enable proper SEO.

Examples of HTML tags are:

Title tag: In the title of the page and it reads as - <Title>Your Title Here</Title>

Example: Internet Explorer

The image depicted here shows the title tag of the web site on top of the window. How you insert your title-tag depends entirely on your needs and requirements. Ensure that you are using appropriate title tags to optimize your web pages.
Firefox:

H1 tags

High-level tags are also very critical for your web pages and you should insert your keywords in your H1 headings and in HTML tags.

For example, HI tag may look like as follows: <h1>High-Level Heading</h1>

Anchor tags

Anchor tags come very handy when you want to create links to a number of other pages.

These tags can direct the visitors to another destination page within the web site.

An example of Anchor tag is:

<a href="http://www.targetwebsite.com/">Text for link</a>

Example:

Links

Ensure that the links inserted in the website relate to the content published in the page. The links listed must allow an internet user to navigate to the active or real web sites. Never abuse the sanctity of links and make sure that links are not broken in your web site. One of the inferior techniques of making your site SEO enabled is propagating link farming. Google does not like link farming and it may ban all those sites that resort to it.

Popularity

How popular is your site? The number of times internet users click on your web site by using Google search engine could be an important criteria.

Your web site will go higher up in ranking list, when a large number of people search for your web site and then click on it to check the web site contents. One of the most important factors of SEO is to enhance the popularity of your web site by participating in forums, blog sites and by publishing a useful newsletter.

Learning web site optimization

The important goal of SEO is to make your site search engine compliant, so that a major search engine like Google can easily retrieve your web site ahead of other sites.

Domain-naming tips

Before you register your domain name, you will need to ensure that the name is SEO friendly and related to the overall theme of your web site.

In the past, hundreds of SEO friendly domains were sold for overwhelming amounts to the tune of millions of dollars.

Let us take this example:

Let us say that you are in the business of selling fresh flowers to online customers. You want to create a new online shopping web site to sell your flowers. Before buying a new domain name, you will want to check the search engine for a good domain name.

When you type the keyword "fresh flowers" in the search bar of Google, the search engine will return a number of results. In the search results page, you can notice that all top search pages have a domain name almost similar to the theme and objective of the business.

Ensure that you are buying a domain name that sounds almost similar to the overall theme or idea of your business. Make sure that the selected domain name contains a good keyword related to the business theme as well.

Here are some more valuable tips:

- ✓ Let the name be as short as possible.
- ✓ Limit the number of characters in the name to about 35 to 40
- ✓ As far as possible, avoid characters like dashes, hyphens and underscores.
- ✓ Choose a .com name. Users always think about a .com name than any other extensions.
- ✓ .com names occupy most of the top pages of Google.

The factor of usability

Internet users want to visit a site that really works for them. They are not interested in a web site that contains broken links and wrongly included pages. The usability factors of a web site are very important, while you consider SEO techniques for your web site.

Let your home page be very simple and effective. Make the rest of the pages in resonance with the home page. Fast loading pages, quick graphics and very good content are the hallmarks of very good and SEO friendly web sites.

Internal and external navigation are also very critical for the success of your SEO campaign. Internal navigation means navigating through different pages of your web site, while external navigation means you are going away from your web site to other related web site that provides extra information to the user. Text based navigation works better for making your site SEO-worthy.

Crawlers find navigating through text based links very easy, while buttons and bars can be quite difficult for a crawler to learn and understand.

You may also need to include text-based keywords within the content inserted on different pages. Anchor tags inserted within the pages will make easy for crawlers to go through different pages of your site.

Tip: Ensure that navigational links that you include are both user and SEO friendly.

You may also need to test your web site several times before releasing it for internet users. SEO is the direct result of lot of people paying a return visit to your web site.

Whatever you do, ensure that many people visit your web site, which will make your web site extremely search engine friendly.

What are the parameters of a SEO friendly web site?

SEO does not occur by accident nor does it come to you without working ceaselessly for hour's non-stop. Just understand that a search engine like Google keeps looking for a number of parameters and factors that are so essential for proper SEO implementation.

Web designing principles are as critical as SEO itself; ensure that you are using the basic principles of SEO, while you are designing and constructing the web site.

Entry and exit pages are also quite important for proper SEO. An internet user may land on your web site, by checking any of the pages embedded within the site.

An internet user may visit the last page first and home page last just before leaving the web site. Internet users can also come to your web site by clicking on a link listed in a different web site.

However, entry pages or home pages are possibly the most important pages of your web site. It is on this page, where most of the site visitors tend to enter and look at your pages.

You may direct your visitors by inserting text based navigation links to visit all other pages; it is just like a gateway through which one can enter a city to visit all the tourist spots.

However, you may also need to identify all those pages that can act as potential entry pages. Once you detect and identify a particular page, you can make it SEO friendly, by applying the best techniques and methods.

Tip: Ensure that you are keeping your entry page up-to-date by reviewing the SEO structure; you can use Google Analytics to check your entry page from time to time.

On the other hand, exit pages are those pages, from where an internet user makes an exit from your site, either by bookmaking your site or just closing the browser window.

They are as critical and important as entry pages, when you are tweaking your web site for SEO. Exit pages are quite important because of two reasons:

- ✓ To lure site visitors from the entry page to a desired exit page.
- ✓ To help Google spiders look through your links in an efficient manner.

Tip: A path is a road on which an internet user navigates through your site. Here is a classical path of a typical web site:

Home – Products – Fresh Flowers – Orchids – Red Type – Description Page – Shopping Cart- Check Out – Payment Page – Receipt – Thank You Page

Note: The above-mentioned example relates to a typical business transaction carried out by a customer.

Here, *Home* is the entry page, while *Thank You* is the exit page. A typical internet user always follows a well-defined path, either to come back to previous pages of just exit through a well-defined exit page.

The magic of powerful titles

Page titles are the other important factors that can largely influence how Google search spider can work on your web site. Google crawlers have the habit of examining the page titles first before checking other elements.

Google search spiders can evaluate the merit of page titles of your web site, before indexing and ranking them in their search directory.

Here are some basic considerations that your SEO campaign must address before submitting the site for search directory:

- ✓ Never ever, use your business name in the title page.
- ✓ Use a descriptive keyword to highlight your title; let the keyword be short and informative
- ✓ Use short page titles with less than 50 characters.
- ✓ Never repeat keywords in the title tags because Google can consider this as a spam.

✓ You can always consider adding some special characters at the starting point or end of the title. These could be a simple inverted comma, a descriptive () or even a set of asterisk.
✓ Generate a sense of excitement in the title tag! Cajole your visitor to take a definite action, when he or she sees the tile tag.

Note: Ensure that you are tagging all page titles when you code and write your web pages.

For example: <title>A Descriptive Web Site Title</title>

The power of meaningful content

Web site content is another important and sensitive element of your web site. Good content means better SEO. Good content always starts with better and meaningful keywords and phrases. Make sure that you are limiting the selection of keywords and phrases to about five or six. Keyword stuffing is a negative technique and Google may take a serious note of keyword stuffing.

A serious problem, it could even result in banning of your web site.

Note: Keyword density is the term used to define the total number of keywords used in a page or within an article.

Keyword densities stipulated for a number of search engines are very low, while Google insists on a keyword density of around 5%.

Fresh and updated content is an important consideration for proper SEO. Blogs are one good example of providing good and fresh content to your web site. More focused content is yet another idea to empower your website.

Changing web pages with free articles, including news clippings and incorporating discussion forums are some other methods than can enhance and tweak your web site.

Including dynamic content may result in broken links; be careful while inserting pages containing dynamic content. You may also like to compliment text pages with interesting and vibrant graphics and images.

If you feel that images and graphics are mandatory for your web site, then you can consider the following suggestions:

Tip: Use tagged graphics for your web site. Tag the image with alt tags inside the Img tags. Here, alt tags are HTML tags that try to display alternative text in presence of graphics or images.

On the other hand, alt tags should be very short, but self-explanatory about the images inserted on web pages. Img tags will result in coded images that will appear on web pages.

Here is an example:

<img src="pic1.jpg" alt="alternative text"/> Where, Image tag = <img src="image1.jpg" and alternative text tag = alt="alternative text"/>

You can perform tagging operation with two main reasons in mind:

Spiders usually fail to analyze simple image files and to evaluate them for SEO. The Google spider can only look at the image and later proceed straight to the text content.

Thus, you should replace that image with relevant text in the form of alternative text to allow the spider to analyze all images. When the alternative text includes important keywords and the image is immediately next to the text, you can optimize your pages for images as well.

Image based search engines can act efficiently to index image based web sites. However, this is still a new and emerging concept.

The problem of frames

Some web sites tend to use frames to highlight and display their content and information. Webmasters use frames to demarcate or segregate the web pages into separate sections each with its own URLs.

However, they can pose a severe compatibility problem with some browsers. As a result, Google spiders will usually find it very difficult to index and rank such sites, especially when they are incompatible or incongruent with some browsers.

Here are some SEO tips, when you are using a web site embedded with a number of frames:

Inserting *noframe* tag to the web site: This tag will help the browser to display and exhibit the site without the framed navigational system. What users see and observe is a stripped and bare-bone version of the web site that is just enough for the user to read and understand the content. Make sure that you are inserting the *noframe* tag code between opening tag and close tag of the entire web site.

Identical content: Ensure that you are including identical content in both *noframe* tags and frame set. In absence of such content on your web pages, Google will assume that you are spamming, while the penalty for such an action could be quite severe and harsh.

Display of an internal page: Search engines can display an internal page of a web site in response to a search query. In absence of a valid link to a menu or home page, an internet user may be stuck with that page.

As a result, navigating to other pages becomes almost impossible. It also means that the crawler will fail to go beyond that page, which eventually results in a failed SEO attempt.

The best possible solution to prevent such a problem is to insert a link that helps you navigate to the home page.

You can include a tag called TARGET = "_top" to help prevent your site from being cocooned within the web site frames. This will help Google crawlers to navigate through the entire web site without any hassles.

The link back to your home page may read as follows:

<a href="index.html" TARGET = "_top">Return to Home Page</a>

SEO strategies and methods may not really work for a framed web site for most obvious reasons. However, you can still try your best to include necessary and well-placed tags to help Google crawler to index and rank your site.

Cookies are becoming an integral part of big web sites, and cookies are the small pieces of codes embedded within the web site. When internet site users access the web site, the stored cookies will become easy to access and later help execute their preferences and choices.

Cookies can be very good and practical tools for web sites that are looking to provide the best to internet users. Some web sites ask the internet user to accept and execute prompts to allow cookies to access the site.

When you enable these prompts and if the user does not use the prompt code to accept the cookies, the search spider will stop at that point and it will never pick up from where is stopped, once the cookies are stopped by the internet user.

The general tip suggested here is to avoid designated prompt query function on the web page, just before the web site delivers the cookie prompt function to the internet user.

Using several programming languages

Java Scripts

You can create dynamic content by using this language. However, Java could be a difficult language for search engine optimization. Java can stop Google crawler from indexing your web site. In fact, Java scripts can impede the growth of your web site vis-à-vis SEO.

However, you can use a different technique to overcome this problem; developers of Java web sites use a method that externalizes all Java scripts included in the web pages. A web server is an external source from where you can execute Java scripts.

Flash language

Flash is a heavy and resource hungry program that consumes lot of critical system resources. A typical flash home page loads very slowly and an internet user cannot navigate to the next page, unless the page is completely loaded.

Flash-based web sites are very difficult to optimize, because Google crawler finds it very difficult to index and rank such web sites. If you are a newbie and busy designing your web site, you may wish to avoid using this language script.

Dynamic ASP

Web sites designed with this language are often very difficult to optimize, just like creating dynamic web pages.

Google crawlers never index or rank most of the dynamic web pages, unless webmasters convert dynamic URLs into effective static URLs.

PHP

This is another language, which does not belong to normal and conventional web site designing practices. Search engine will not be able to index and rank your PHP based web site.

However, you can overcome this problem by designing the site to look like an ordinary HTML web site.

Other common concerns

As a webmaster, you are bound to face a number of problems and obstacles, while optimizing your web site for SEO. Some are very easy to overcome, while the others could prove a big nuisance.

Here are some of those problems:

Domain Cloaking

Domain cloaking means creating an efficiently optimized web site just for developing SEO. Nevertheless, such sites could be actually useless to a site visitor, though the site looks absolutely gorgeous and pleasing. Intelligent web masters use this dark method to optimize their web site. However, Google can easily make out such sites and delete the site from their directories.

Duplicate content

Webmasters have a tendency to include content purchased from others for inclusion in their web sites.

The quality of content used to populate web sites could be useless and scrap; including such content may raise serious issues with Google servers. Most content-driven web sites use and insert free articles and reports from content generation sites.

In fact, thousands of web sites can publish the similar articles or reports at the same time. In fact, this can create a lot of problem for Google search engine servers.

Google crawlers look out for four different types of duplicate content:

Articles distributed for publication in hundreds of web site: If you observe carefully, you can notice that hundreds of web sites publish the same type of content.

Free article submission directories provide free content in the form of articles and reports to interested web publishers who want to publish content on their web sites. Ensure that you are avoiding free content provided by marketing perceptive web sites that keep looking for promoting their own web sites.

E-commerce portals that publish product descriptions: Product descriptions published on e commerce stores may not be crawled and indexed in Google search engine servers. Google crawlers avoid product descriptions, because a big e-commerce web site can contain thousands of such descriptions.

Copied web pages: Google may not index such web pages, because it has a strict policy of rejecting plagiarized pages and contents.

Content scrapping: Content scrapping is copying content from other web sites and editing it in an efficient manner, so that it looks different and fresh.

Post web site publication management

Soon after publishing a SEO enabled web site, you will need to work on it continuously to keep the optimization intact and updated. You may also need to work ceaselessly to keep optimizing the web site for better ranking and indexing.

Some of the post management strategies could include the following:

Content thieves

Stolen content is a big problem among those webmasters, who practice black-hat SEO methods to optimize their web sites. By including carefully chosen codes and tags, you can easily find out who is stealing our contents.

Tagging method works very well to detect and catch content thieves. You can also use it to control domain-cloaked web sites, who are stealing your content for online publication.

Continuous changes and updates to the web site

People tend to believe that once they optimize their web sites, it remains there forever. However, with frequent updates and content changes, the basic structure of your web site may undergo a drastic change. There may be broken links that do not work, or a number of invisible problems can derail your SEO campaign. Search rankings and indexing may also change and undergo transformations in a drastic and negative manner, if you fail to optimize your site on a consistent basis.

SEO is a very complex thing to follow and practice, and you will need to use and employ your personal time and energy to keep your site under tight check.

Keywords and SEO

Keywords and SEO always go hand in hand and without good keywords, you may never realize your SEO goals and objectives. Keywords are those little, precious tools that help a search spider to search, index and rank a web site.

Choosing the right set of keywords is a thing of fine art. SEO consultants spend hours and hours of energy and time to choose the best keywords for a web site.

Using relevant and popular keywords can help your web site achieve better ranking and come up on the top most pages of the search engines.

Why keywords are so important?

With the right type of keywords, you can achieve many good things, out of which SEO is the most cherished one. A potential web site visitor will type-in required keywords into the search bar of Google search engine to retrieve a series of web sites in the form of search pages.

If you match the keyword search preference of a site visitor with your own good keywords, you can expect him or her to visit your site.

Here are some important examples:

Let us say that you want to buy some fresh flowers through an online portal. Now, you want to use Google search engine for the purpose. Let us assume that you will type a niche keyword like "flowers" on the search bar of the search engine.

Now, Google will return thousands of pages of all those web sits that sell or provide information about flowers.

However, it may never be possible to search through all those thousands of web pages clogging the big web world. Now, let us say that you change your search method by entering a slightly changed keyword, from "flowers" to "fresh flowers".

The ensuing search result pages are very few and it becomes quite easy to find what you want from those few web pages.

Tip: Choosing the right type of keywords will help you find top most position on the Google search pages. Remember that a majority of site visitors use keywords to go their preferred web sites.

Here are some general tips:

1. Ask very simple questions as to why keywords are so important for SEO. What are the designated functions and activities of keywords?

2. Who wants the products and services that your web site offers?

3. What will an internet user think, when he or she wants to find something on the search engine?

4. What kind of keyword variations and changes can a site visitor use, while searching for some products, services or information?

5. How does Google search engine act and perform, when a site visitor forwards a search query to Google?

6. What is the basic nature and characters of a niche keyword that can bring in lot of traffic to your web site?

7. Why webmasters die for very high paying and niche keywords?

How to use heuristics

Heuristics are quite critical for SEO, as it can help you introduce subtle variations in the manner site visitors search for a particular keyword or phrase. Let us assume the following scenario: Let us say that you are running an online portfolio that sells fresh flowers. When an internet surfer is searching for fresh flowers, the Google spider will try to visit as many sites as possible by using varied keywords, phrases and their keyword densities. While searching for web sites, the Google spider will also provide a score based on a number of considerations, like keyword relevancy and page optimization. Let us say that a user wants to find fresh red orchid flowers. When he or she types this query with a series of keywords, the spider tends to separate the search query words based on the context of the search.

The search pages extracted may also be out of context and relevancy. Furthermore, the results returned in the search may not relate to the intended search, that is buying fresh flowers.

Google will also search for links that are useful and relevant for the user, who wants to buy fresh flowers. When you insert irrelevant links in your web site, then Google will consider that you are using link farming technique to optimize your web site.

On the flipside, if you include relevant and the right type of links related to fresh flowers, Google will then crawl efficiently through your web site to index and rank your site on top of the search engines.

What is anchor text?

Anchor text is the linked text that you include in your web site. It appears as cleanly underlined or colored words on your web pages and anchor text provide links to another web page, either inside the web site or to a different web site (external) page. Inserting anchor text in your web pages offers you a number of advantages.

Search spiders can easily locate the anchor text links that lead to other web pages.

These links will tell you what your web site is all about and how it plans to disseminate useful information to internet users. With anchor text inserted in carefully selected locations, you can enhance the validity of keywords as well as those of anchor texts. However, when you over-optimize your web site with too many anchor text links, Google may decide to ban your site altogether for reasons already known to you.

Google bombing is a technique, when a webmaster deliberately includes a word or phrase in every anchor text line with intent to appear high up in the Google search pages.

Tip: Ensure that you are using anchor text with intelligent keywords embedded, so that Google crawlers enter through these links to visit other pages within the main website and later to pages located outside.

Anchor text relates very closely to important keywords and when used properly, they can help you optimize your web site in a proper manner.

Keywords are very important and critical for proper SEO implementation and they form the firm foundation on which you can optimize your web pages.

Fact: The type or quality of keywords that you insert in your web site plays a large role.

How do you know that some keywords are good?

Selecting the right keywords can take your web site very high to the first page of search engine, while wrong selection means your web site working as a non-starter and a big failure.

There are two types of keywords:

1. Branded keywords are those that are closely associated with your business brand of theme.

2. Generic keywords: These important keywords are not associated with your business brand or theme.

Furthermore, there are two more varieties of keywords:

1. Keywords that come to you with a fee attached to them. These keywords belong to pay-per-click method of marketing.

2. Natural organic keywords you can find with your own individual effort and later inserted on your web pages for normal search by internet users.

The main difference between these two types of keywords is that you will purchase the former, while the latter one is free, but inserted after careful planning and consideration.

The best way to select organic keywords is to evaluate your business objectives and link any selected keywords to the business themes.

Whatever the keywords you chose for your business, ensure that they are specific and targeted.

Here are some simple examples of broad and specific keywords:

Broad	Specific
Fresh flowers	Fresh seasonal flowers
Orchid flowers	Thai orchid flowers
Annual flowers	Annual phlox flowers

Tip: Ensure that you are choosing specific keywords with important phrases sprinkled in between.

Keyword density and SEO

It is very difficult to quantify or suggest the exact numbers of keywords that you want to insert in the web page. Keyword density is a measure of total number of keywords that occur on a web page, vis-à-vis the number of words on a page. Each search engine has its own keyword density requirement.

Google stipulates that you can insert keywords at the maximum level of about 5%. Assessing what is the right percentage for your web site is up to your discretion and wishes.

In many cases, keyword density is just one of the factors that co-exist with many other elements.

You will need to develop a keen acumen to decide the keyword density measurement for your web site. On the other hand, very high keyword density means that you are stuffing too many numbers of keywords with in a web page, which can eventually affect your search engine ranking.

Why organic keywords are good?

You can make use of the benefits offered by organic keywords to optimize your web site for search engines. However, using organic keywords may take a long time to appear on top of the search engine like Google.

Most of the webmasters who are working on SEO techniques combine the goodness of organic keywords with that of practicality of PPC keywords. This will ensure them that their web sites are optimized to the best of their abilities; in fact, this method ensures that their web sites appear on top of the Google search engine much faster and within a short span of two or three months. First, you should know more about organic keywords that you wish to include in your web site.

Make efforts to understand what they are and how you can work to tweak your web pages. You can use a website metric application provided by Google to learn more about organic keywords. You can easily find out the overall merit of using such keywords. Another way to find out the feasibility of using organic keywords is to check the keywords that relate to the theme of your business, its products or services. Let us say that you are dealing with an online business that sells flowers.

Now, you may consider a number of keywords related to your business theme and choose some of them for your website. However, it is not all necessary to choose a keyword or keywords like "flowers" or "flower" because you have already embedded them in the web pages.

However, you can choose a number of other keywords in combination or tandem, so that the overall effectiveness of optimization becomes more pronounced. Carefully chosen and executed organic keywords can help you in setting up an effective SEO technique.

Pay-per-Click and SEO

SEO and PPC campaigns go hand in hand and in close partnership in optimizing your website. Per se, PPC is not a mandatory requirement to tweak your website for best optimization. Hundreds of PPC services are available in the market.

However, you will need to choose the one that fulfills your needs and requirements. Google PPC is possibly the best of them and it can work very well for your web site in an efficient manner.

The main objective of using a PPC is to drive and import traffic to your site. More traffic means better search engine ranking. However, you may need more than just traffic, while assessing your site's ability to reach the top of the search engines.

PPC programs offer you a number of advantages over conventional SEO programs:

1. You need not change the basic structure of your web site nor do you need to add or delete or modify any code structure of your web site.

2. Implementing and using PPC is very easy and simple. In that way, you can easily integrate basic SEO principles along with PPC to start straightaway.

PPC can have some sort of negative influence on your SEO program in the following manner:

1. When you pay for an automated listing program, it may actually reduce the rank of your keyword related SEO efforts.

2. Some experts still believe that PPC does not exert any influence on your SEO efforts. Organic keywords can play an important role in pushing your web site higher up in the page ranking.

3. PPC stresses on some selected keywords that may cost you a lot. However, not all selected and paid keywords could work for your web site.

Tip: If you want to use a paid PPC program for your SEO program, you can combine the power of organic keywords to enhance the overall effect of SEO.

How to tag your web site

Tagging your web site is an important activity that you must consider before aspiring to make your web site an instant hit in the Google search engine.

Site tagging is perhaps the most useful and sensitive techniques that you can use to optimize your website.

The tags that you insert tell lot of stories about your web site and its structure than your content will tell them. Mind you, HTML tags always face the crawler's navigation direction and the relationship between the Google spiders and tags is very intricate and close.

Though content included in your web site is very important, tags play a different role altogether. Before site visitors get to see your web site, you must ensure proper detour of your HTML tags by the Google crawler.

If you ask why HTML tagging is so important, I can say that it is everything.

By large, your site works wonderfully well on Google search engine, when you insert the tags that can efficiently control your web site almost silently in the background.

How does tagging work for you?

Tagging is inserting the right type of HTML commands at the right places. The type of tags you include depends entirely on your needs and requirements.

Tip: You may include any type of tags depending on the structure of the web site, but what is important and crucial is how you format your tags.

For example, when you insert container tags, you must ensure that you have both opening and closing tags in the page code.

Opening tag = Bracketed with two sharp brackets (<tag>).

Closing bracket = Almost the same, but it includes a slash before the tag to indicate that the container is closing (</tag>).

Note that the tag name repeats in both of the tags. This will inform the Google crawler more about the tag commands, where they start and close. When you use the Bold tag, just the words inserted between the opening and closing tags will become formatted with a bold font; here, you are not formatting the entire page.

On the other hand, CSS or Cascading Style Sheets is not exactly a coding or tagging method. It is a formatting method used to enhance the look and feel of your web site.

When you use this technique, you must also ensure that you are making other tags work in a proper manner. When the crawlers actually run through your web site, they can easily see the tags embedded in the style sheets.

Extra HTML tags

NoFollow tag: One of the first tags you should use is the *nofollow tag*. This tag is represented by a snippet of code called <rel="nofollow"> which is an attribute that informs a search engine spider to avoid visiting a certain link on your web site.

Though this tag is not a specific tool to optimize your site, you can still use it to enhance certain features of your web site.

Strong and emphasis

If you are looking to format text on the web pages, how do you format bold and italic words? If you are planning your website, you may wish to consider including CSS formatting method. When you format your text by making it bold, your users will definitely read it, but search spiders will never be able to see and evaluate it; Google spider will just see the tag, but it will fail to recognize the bold effect.

You may also use better HTML tags like:

<strong>strong</strong> and
<em>emphasis </em> tags.

Now, the <strong> tag will become bold, while the <em> will turn into italics type of formatting. When you include these tags, the search spiders will pay immediate attention to the marked words that are included within the containers.

<noframes> tag is another critical tag that will make your framed web site appears non-framed and normal to Google spiders. However, this may not offer you a complete solution to your SEO efforts.

Here is a brief summary of what you should include as tags in your web site:

Normal Page	Frame Page	Frame Page with <noframes> Tag
<HTML>	<HTML>	<HTML>
<Head>	<Head>	<Head>
<Title>Page Title</Title>	<Title>Page Title</Title>	<Title>Page Title</Title>
</Head>	</Head>	</Head>
<Body>	<Frameset>	<Frameset>
Body Text goes here	Frame Code goes here	<Frameset cols="25%,*">
</Body>	</Frameset>	<Frame SRC="nav.html">
</HTML>	</HTML>	<Frame SRC="display.html">
		</Frameset>
		<Noframes>
		Alternative HTML goes here
		</noframes>
		</HTML>

Acronyms and abbreviations

You may also like to use an acronym and abbreviation tag like <acronym> or <abbr> to inform Google spider that you are using these tags in your web site.

When you assign acronyms and abbreviations as your keywords on your web page, the text in its entirety can only be glanced by the spider rather than just the letters mentioned in the acronyms and abbreviations.

Here are the examples of these tags:

Acronym tags:

<acronym title="Search Engine Optimization">SEO</acronym>

Abbreviation Tags:

<abbr title="United States of America">USA</abbr>

How do you use redirection pages to optimize your web site?

Another element of a web site, it plays an important role in search engine optimization. The method and mode in which you use redirected pages can adversely influence your search engine ranking. There are two types of page redirection - one is permanent, while the other is temporary. The type of redirection pages used can have tremendous effect over your SEO efforts.

You can have three main types of page redirects:

301 Redirect: It is a permanent type of redirect, where the page is redirected from one page to the other, within the website or one page to another web site.

302 Redirect: A temporary redirect page that takes web site users from one web site to the other. You may not have an access to the original web page when you remove the redirect page code, which eventually makes the internet user travel back to the original site.

404 Error Page: This redirection takes the internet user to page that shows an error. This message could be "This page is no longer available, please check the URL and try again or use the refresh button on your browser."

Tip: Google spider can read a redirected page as per the number specified on the web page. You may wish to employ each of these numbers under different contexts.

301 Redirect: Use when you make the web pages migrate from one URL to another.

302 Redirect: Use this number when you have a temporary web site running and when you want to your visitors to see this page.

404 Redirect: Use it when you want to indicate an error.

Tip: Webmasters often commit an error to include wrong page redirection, when they optimize their web sites for SEO. Ensure that you are using the right type of number, so that you are exporting the traffic to the other sites, to where you are planning your internet users to navigate.

What is search engine spam?

Search engine spam is perhaps the most difficult problem that Google search engine can face. Search engine spamming can also become a big nuisance for the webmaster who is handling the SEO campaign.

Search engine spam is:

Web pages designed and created to deceive the search engine to provide doubtful, bad quality and useless search results. You may need to avoid search engine spamming at any cost. If you propagate search spamming beyond a certain limit, Google will penalize you severely and the resultant punishment could be an immediate delisting from the search engine.

What are doorway pages?

An internet user may confuse a doorway page along with a landing page. However, they are not even close to a standard landing page. Webmasters create doorway pages that mislead search engine to help increase the search engine ranking of web sites.

Doorway pages are almost like redirection pages that eventually take the site visitors to another web site; webmasters incorporate some deceiving techniques like very quick Meta tag refresh or Java scripts or even server-side redirection scripts.

What are hidden and tiny texts?

In the past, webmasters used to incorporate hidden and tiny text blocks to derive search engine ranking. Webmasters can insert keyword rich text that resembles the identical color and shade of the background.

A typical site visitor cannot see the embedded text, but Google spiders can easily make it out even you are hiding the text by using the most advanced page coding techniques.

This practice is illegal and the penalty for the offense is a certain delisting from the directory. The offense becomes more serious and heinous when you use keyword-stuffing techniques along with hidden texts.

What is SEO over submission?

A number of web masters submit the URL's of their web site by using an automated method. However, there are chances that automated submission services may submit the URLs a number of times within a span of one or two months.

Ensure that you are not using the technique of over-submission to seek immediate listing on Google search engines. Use the manual method to submit your URL after reading the submission guidelines with care.

What is page jacking?

Page jacking is yet another dubious method that is almost similar to content scrapping. Page jacking refers to copying of pages of entire web site just for enhancing search engine ranking and generating traffic to your other sites.

The ultimate penalty for page jacking is criminal prosecution, plagiarism, trademark violation, patent violation and finally permanent delisting from the search engines.

What is bait and switch?

It is a method of SEO for creating a highly optimized web page specifically for achieving higher page ranking. Soon after optimizing the pages for SEO, the webmaster of the site may replace the pages of the optimized site with those that are normal and less optimized. However, this technique may not work in the longer run, as Google has the habit of crawling over your site from time to time and in a coordinated manner.

Special SEO techniques for different types of web sites

Web sites come in many forms and types; there are hundreds of different web sites based on techniques used, languages, scripts and themes. Creating SEO techniques for multi-lingual web sites is actually very tough and time consuming. You may need to use highly advanced techniques to optimize your web sites created in different languages.

If you have a web site in a different language, you can consider optimizing the web site in the language used on the site.

Here are some simple guidelines that you can use to optimize your multilingual sites:

- ✓ Translate the keywords into the language of the web site. In some cases, you may also need to use a new set of keywords.
- ✓ Translate the existing web content into the new language: You may need to solicit the professional help of translator to get your translation performed.
- ✓ Employ similar SEO rules and regulations: You can use the same set of SEO rules and regulations to optimize your multilingual sites.
- ✓ Incorporate proper and normal links: Ensure that proper links are included in both the English version, as well as the multilingual ones. In multilingual web sites, you may need to provide an English version to enable English-speaking internet users to understand the meaning of links.
- ✓ Insert language switchover icons easily readable by the site visitors.

Managing a web site that boasts of hundreds of pages of content is quite difficult and strenuous. To handle and manage such sites, you may want to use an efficient content management system that can index and arrange pages as per your wishes and demands.

Content Management Tool is a utility that helps you design, create, publish, manage, discover, find, invent and distribute content for your web site.

Most of the paid and open source CMS systems are efficient and organized. They are also extremely SEO friendly. However, before using a CMS, you may need to ask yourself a series of questions about its efficacy and usability factors in relation to web site SEO.

Optimization for Google Search Engines

In essence, page optimization for all major search engines is almost similar. However, what they look for and seek while they are searching is entirely different. Each of these search engines is different in the manner of seeking information and details from the web site.

This book has already given you a brief idea of how Google works and behaves in its operation. You should also understand a few more things about Google and its search mechanism. These practical tips will tell you how you can optimize your site further to enhance the site ranking.

Tip: If your web site still exists on the web world with at least one or two links associated with it, your site will definitely crawled in all certainty. Be patient enough to wait for the Google to crawl over you web site.

Google never sells page position for money! You have to find your way on to the top of the search engine with your hard work and dedication.

The only time when Google collaborates with you in a commercial meaning is when you pay for their AdWords program.

What is Pagerank?

Google is legendary for its ability to index and rank millions and millions of web sites. Its high-ranking algorithm is the practical and efficient tool that measures the ranking ability of your web site by taking into account a number of parameters and elements related to the web pages. An element of that algorithm is the now famous Google PageRank!

According to Google, Pagerank is:

"PageRank relies on the uniquely democratic nature of the Web by using its vast link structure as an indicator of an individual page's value.

In essence, Google interprets a link from page A to page B as a vote, by page A, for page B. However, Google looks at considerably more than the sheer volume of votes, or links a page receives; for example, it also analyzes the page that casts the vote.

Votes cast by pages that are themselves "important" weigh more heavily and help to make other pages "important."

Using these and other factors, Google provides its views on pages' relative importance. Of course, important pages mean nothing to you if they do not match your query. Therefore, Google combines PageRank with sophisticated text-matching techniques to find pages that are both important and relevant to your search.

Google goes far beyond the number of times a term appears on a page and examines dozens of aspects of the page's content (and the content of the pages linking to it) to determine if it's a good match for your query."

In all practical purposes, Google PageRanking depends on a secret ballot system that tries to compare your web pages with all other web pages in the web world. This secret comparison will help Google to choose those pages that are very relevant for a normal search performed based on a number of critical elements.

Tip: It is an indicator of how well your web site performs in comparison to others. A simple web page that is linked (in and out) by a number of web pages may get a high ranking.

In absence of such links, your page ranking may be very low. Please visit: Google's webmasters page at http://www.google.com/intl/en/webmasters

Some of the other useful tools are:

Site Status Wizard: You can find out whether your site is indexed by Google or not.

Webmaster tools: Google provides a number of different tools that are critical for SEO. You can find a very good site map generator here.

Content submission tools: You can use these tools to submit your site to the search engine. You can also add products and content to the Book Search.

Webmaster blog: You can participate in the forum to seek solutions to your problems.

You will also find a number of useful information and details about Google's policies and issues.

Webmaster discussion groups: Talk to other people here, to know and collect advanced information about SEO.

Help center: Help center provides you timely tips and suggestions for all nagging problems.

Tracking and Tuning your web site for SEO

SEO implementation is a continuous process that needs your time and effort as well as money. In addition, an interactive and iterative process, it needs a 24x7 monitoring and evaluation. You will also need to check all the vital and definitive parameters and elements that act as the lifelines for proper SEO.

The set of data that you cull or extract from Google Analytics is just like an account balance statement, while the information collected from this useful center is extremely helpful in finding valid solutions to your SEO problem.

Here are some steps that you can employ to track the progress of SEO, as well as tune it to perform better:

Google Analytics

This is one of the best tools available on the web to help you set in motion an efficient SEO plan. It is a mandatory tool for all webmasters as well!

In general, this tool provides you the following features:

- ✓ Visitor tracking (new and repeat),
- ✓ Source of traffic like derived from search engines and referrals
- ✓ Visitor trends
- ✓ User behavior
- ✓ Index patterns
- ✓ Index history

Tip: All the above-mentioned information and details are possible when you use and place a simple and effective Java script near the footer of your web site pages.

Installing Google Analytics tools

Installing Google Analytics is very simple and straightforward. Go to Google Analytics page and register by using your Google account. Now, enter your URL of the site that you want Google to track and report you.

Google lets you insert a unique Java snip-let for each of your web pages. When the tracking begins, you can collect lot of information on your web site by using this code.

Google Analytics runs very silently in the background without disturbing anything. Here are some of the types of reports that Google generates for you:

Basic keyword reporting

Google can record keywords and phrases used in every page of your web site. It can also find out more about referrals made to your web site by using keywords and phrases. With the results obtained, you can easily find out those terms that need further tweaking and optimization.

A useful function offered here is how people find your site and in what manner they work to come to your site. You can access this feature by going to Traffic courses and to Keywords menu function.

Tracking customer

Internet users have their own journey pattern, while making visits to a particular web site.

This journey can be broken down into four different steps:

Landing page: Some site visitors will directly type the URL of your web site to reach the home page. On the other hand, a number of other users may enter your home page through either a PPC engine or an affiliate site. They can also enter your web site through an inbound link from other web sites.

Funnel Path: Funnels are those specific paths where you expect your site visitor to visit your site and help you achieve some of your SEO goals. It is also the process of taking your users from your landing page to other useful web pages.

Money page: It is the page where an internet user gets an opportunity to help you reach one of your important goals. It could be a sign up or even a download.

Goal completion: Once an internet user helps you reach a goalpost, you may need to send him or her *thank you* note inserted in the last web page. Let us think of an example:

Let us say that you are dealing with selling fresh flowers through your online portal.

We will also presume that you have purchased some links by subscribing two famous e-zines with plenty of traffic. Let us say that you have paid a total of $1000 for these links and now you want to track the overall performance and ROI of both of these links.

In fact, the paid links actually point to a specific landing page within the web site solely designed for the purpose of SEO campaign. On that page, you want to attract more customers by providing a mouth-watering 50% rebate on some of the products.

Here are some important steps that you consider while optimizing your site:

1. You can insert a campaign tracking parameter in the link:

```
<a href="http://www.freshflowers.com/seasonal-flowers-half-priceoffer html?utm_medium=paidlinks&utm_campaign=ezines" rel="nofollow">50% off seasonal flowers</a>
```

Note that you are including a *"nofollow"* link parameter in the embedded link. When you include this link, it is certain that Google will not follow the link to that page or take into consideration this link, when evaluating your site for page ranking.

You may perform this action for two main reasons: First, you may want to escape harsh penalty from Google for buying links. Secondly, you do not want Google to index your pages, as the page that you design includes codes that are readable only by the site visitors.

You can easily firm up this by telling spiders not to index your page; in fact, you are using a disallow command in your site robots.txt file.

The next obvious step suggested is to set up a page in Google Analytics and specify the funnel channel to allow for goal completion by the e-zine readers.

After sometime, you can start assessing the results that are emanating from Google Analytics control panel.

In fact, there are three sectors of useful data:

1. Site referrer statistics: You can observe that there is a visible increase in the traffic generated.

2. Campaign statistics: You can also note the numbers of internet users dispatched from two sites, when compared to other similar campaigns. You can even check the goal conversion data accrued from the said web sites.

3. Site overlay statistics: Here, you can visualize how users are navigating through your different web pages.

This is perhaps the most significant feature of Google Analytics that can help you in your effort to implement SEO campaign.

Google Webmaster Tools

These tools help you in a number of ways:

1. Check and inspect how Googlebot is crawling over your site

2. Check the overall ranking of your web site

3. Check, which one of your links is, clicked most by internet users.

4. Check the anchor text used in your inbound links and see how they are performing

5. See when Google spiders last visited your site

6. Check if there have been any crawling errors

7. Inspect robots.txt file to see how it is performing

8. Apply for a different crawl rate by Google.

9. Create special www preferences for all of your URLs

Under statistics section, you can check a number of factors like:

1. The PageRank profile for all of your web sites

2. Locate top search queries for the sites

3. Locate top search query clicks

4. Most commonly used text in the links that lead to your site

5. Locate most used text lines in your pages

Tip: Under the links section, you can note down the total number of inbound links that exist for each of your pages.

Other useful tools

Tracking Google PageRank (PR):

Download your Google Tool Bar from the site www.toolbar.google.com.

This is perhaps the most demanded and cherished attribute from Google!

The distribution of your PageRank in the web depends on a set and well-defined pattern. This system is in fact a zero-zero game.

How to track keyword performance

You can buy a tool called API key from a third party source to monitor your keyword's performance. Google has stopped providing API key services and you may need to approach other to get one.

Monitoring your traffic rank

Quantifying the incoming traffic and monitoring its inflow is an important task. To retain the page ranking of your web site, you will need to monitor the traffic coming to your site. To monitor your Google search engine ranking, you can use the services of number of useful web sites like:

- ✓ Neilsen NetRatings,
- ✓ ComScore,
- ✓ Hitwise,
- ✓ Alexa Toolbar
- ✓ Google PageRank
- ✓ Amazon SalesRank
- ✓ www.googlerankings.com
- ✓ www.gorank.com
- ✓ www.compete.com

Google tracks and monitors all site visitors by recording their IP addresses. However, this may pose a big problem, Google may not consider site visitors using the same IP addresses (as in an internet browsing center or office computers) as different users.

A successful web site means plenty of site visitors who also make return and repeated visits to your web site.

Tip: One of the visible symbols of a successful SEO campaign is a visible increase in the number of site visitors and accompanying inbound traffic.

Page view or page impression is the total number of people who make a visit your site. You can also find out the average number of visitors per web page as well.

Some site visitors may like a particular page immensely and they keep coming back to that page from time to time. This gives you a very good idea of the perceived popularity of your web pages.

Some visitors may just glance at your web site pages and then leave to another destination. Your SEO efforts must specially focus on these people, who may become your favored, future customers. When you give or provide people what they want through your web pages, your SEO experiment will become huge success.

The key indicator of assessing a site visitor is the referral data; a referrer is the link that your site visitor would click to land on your web pages.

When you calculate the total number of referrals accumulated every month, you can easily evaluate the available data to get a fair idea about your performance, whether it is improving or not.

Keywords can tell a lot about your SEO and its quality. Search terms and strings that appear on the referring URL can tell lot of stories, whether you have inserted proper keywords or not. In fact, juggling with keywords is an art and if you are lucky, you can even strike a goldmine by collecting some of the best keywords in the world.

At times, you may even land some keywords that your competitors might have been looking for so badly! All future SEO activities should depend on all the positive results that you gained from your previous campaign.

The browser section of your internet browser clearly shows which search engine robots and spiders have been visiting your web site.

Another important SEO tip is to reassess and reevaluate the data left by robots and consult the crawler guidance page provided at the robot homepage. Tuning your SEO campaign is one intelligent act and you will need to proceed very cautiously in this regard.

When you try to build lot of links within short time, without introducing significant variations in the nature of anchor text or clickable text links, Google may conclude that you are inducing some unhealthy and unnatural clinking patterns within your web site.

Make sure that you are revisiting your link building activities every quarter of the year depending on the rankings procured.

If you are not achieving your targeted links, you can slowly build them over time and with a systematic approach. Know how to use Google Analytics and other web site statistics and learn how you can improve your SEO campaign.

If your web site is getting enough traffic from an existing keyword phrase, then you can improve your campaign based on that keyword.

Ensure that you are tweaking your keywords from time to time; create a solid keyword analysis of your keywords, so that you can build a steady stream of incoming traffic to your site. Sometimes, the links that you build may not survive for a long time due to some unknown reasons.

Assert that you are building your links every month and on a consistent basis. If you do not work on your links for a long time, you may loose everything that you worked on with so much dedication and effort. It is vital that you are maintaining the position of your SEO by using periodic tuning and maintenance.

Getting on to the top pages of Google search engine is an important business mission. Webmasters can do anything to get on the top two or three pages of Google. Do you know that more than 90% of first time visits by site-visitors are through Google search engine? In fact, more than 60% of site visitors enter your web site pages through one of the Google's proprietary web sites!

Did you also know that as many as 84% of site visitors never go past the second page of search results? In fact, more than 70% of site visitors never click on paid and sponsored results! SEO implementation is a multi-faced activity that needs tremendous amount of skills and intelligence.

It is always time consuming and a costly affair. You may wish to spread and allocate your resources, like time and effort, evenly on a range of activities that focus on SEO practice. Do not waste your time on one single activity and be moderate, while working on a number of simultaneous activities.

SEO implantation is not an end to your business goals, but it is just an important part of your business venture. Make sure that you are using the opportunity with maximum effectiveness. Finally, here are some top tips for your SEO implementation success:

1. Search for a practical niche and business theme and create useful and beneficial content around the theme.

2. Give enough numbers of reasons for your site visitors to come back and make a repeat visit

3. Let your visitors bookmark your site and create a link with other sites.

4. Create a solid strategy and lay the right type of foundation.

5. Ensure that you are hosting your web site with a trustworthy host and guarantee that your site is on the air throughout the year.

6. Employ all available techniques and methods at your disposal and use them in your SEO effort.

7. SEO is also more about legible and high quality copywriting.

8. Spend time while submitting your site by using a manual method and writing very good sales messages and press releases.

9. Establish a hook so that people can latch on to it to visit your site.

10. Use paid advertising method as one of the SEO technique. You can make paid advertizing as a substitute technique to compliment your SEO work. Use an organic approach to take your site all the way up to the top of the search engine.

11. Create decent and working landing pages, and buttress them with equally good entry and exit pages.

12. Use local business directories to market your web sites.

13. Target your web site on regional basis; your may focus at creating a formidable web site for a particular area, locality or region.

14. Allow other users to syndicate your content and products; this will help you accumulate a lot of incoming traffic and links.

15. Participate in blog and community forums to leave your distinctive signature at the end of your posting.

16. Join one of those wonderful social networking sites like Face Book, Stumble Upon, Orkut and My Space to propagate and distribute your business ideas and concepts.

Now that you have you finished reading this small booklet, I believe that you are empowered with all those little, but important secrets and tricks that are required to implement a rock solid and fail-proof SEO plan.

When you employ a series of excellent and result-oriented SEO techniques, you can expect your web pages to rank very high up on the Google search pages. Best wishes!

Obstacles are those frightful things you see
when you take your eyes off your goal.
- Henry Ford

If you enjoyed this book, please look at:

GOOGLE **ADWORDS** ADVANCED 2.0

GOOGLE **ADSENSE** ADVANCED 2.0

These next few pages are for search & book engine purposes only!

Common miss-spelling of the term "Search Engine Optimization"

search engine optimization, searchengine optimization, search engineoptimization, searchengineoptimization, search optimization engine, engine search optimization, engine optimization search, optimization search engine, optimization engine search, earch engine optimization, sarch engine optimization, serch engine optimization, seach engine optimization, searh engine optimization, searc engine optimization, search ngine optimization, search egine optimization, search enine optimization, search engne optimization, search engie optimization, search engin optimization, search engine ptimization, search engine otimization, search engine opimization, search engine optmization, search engine optiization, search engine optimzation, search engine optimiation, search engine optimiztion, search engine optimizaion, search engine optimizaton, search engine optimizatin, search engine optimizatio, esarch engine optimization, saerch engine optimization, serach engine optimization, seacrh engine optimization, searhc engine optimization, search negine optimization, search egnine optimization, search enigne optimization, search engnie optimization, search engien optimization, search engine potimization, search engine otpimization, search engine opitmization, search engine optmiization, search engine optiimzation, search engine optimziation, search engine optimiaztion, search engine optimiztaion, search engine optimizaiton, search engine optimizatoin, search engine optimizatino, ssearch engine optimization, seearch engine optimization, seaarch engine optimization, searrch engine optimization, searcch engine optimization, searchh engine optimization, search eengine optimization, search enngine optimization, search enggine optimization, search engiine optimization, search enginne optimization, search enginee optimization, search engine ooptimization, search engine opptimization, search engine opttimization, search engine optiimization, search engine optimmization, search engine optimiization, search engine optimizzation, search engine optimizaation, search engine optimizattion, search engine optimizatiion, search engine optimizatioon, search engine optimizationn, aearch engine optimization, dearch engine optimization, swarch engine optimization, srarch engine optimization, sesrch engine optimization, seaech engine optimization, seatch engine optimization, searxh engine optimization, searvh engine optimization, searcg engine optimization, searcj engine optimization, search wngine optimization, search rngine optimization, search ebgine optimization, search emgine optimization, search enfine optimization, search enhine optimization, search engune optimization, search engone optimization, search engibe optimization, search engime optimization, search enginw optimization, search enginr optimization, search engine iptimization, search engine pptimization, search engine oprimization, search engine opyimization, search engine optumization, search engine optomization, search engine optinization, search engine optimuzation, search engine optimozation, search engine optimixation, search engine optimizstion, search engine optimizarion, search engine optimizayion, search engine optimizatuon, search engine optimizatoon, search engine optimizatiin, search engine optimizatipn, search engine optimizatiob, search engine optimizatiom, wearch engine optimization, eearch engine optimization, xearch engine optimization, zearch engine optimization, s3arch engine optimization, s4arch engine optimization, sdarch engine optimization, ssarch engine optimization, seqrch engine optimization, sewrch engine optimization, sezrch engine optimization, sea4ch engine optimization, sea5ch engine optimization, seafch engine optimization, seadch engine optimization, seardh engine optimization, searfh engine optimization, searcy engine optimization, searcu engine optimization, searcn engine optimization, searcb engine optimization, search 3ngine optimization, search 4ngine optimization, search dngine optimization, search sngine optimization, search ehgine optimization, search ejgine optimization, search entine optimization, search enyine optimization, search enbine optimization, search envine optimization, search eng8ne optimization, search eng9ne optimization, search engkne optimization, search engjne optimization, search engihe optimization, search engije optimization, search engin3 optimization, search engin4 optimization, search engind optimization, search engins optimization, search engine 9ptimization, search engine 0ptimization, search engine lptimization, search engine kptimization, search engine op5imization, search engine op6imization, search engine opgimization, search engine opfimization, search engine opt8mization, search engine opt9mization, search engine optkmization, search engine optjmization, search engine optijization, search engine optikization, search engine optim8zation, search engine optim9zation, search engine optimkzation, search engine optimjzation, search engine optimiaation, search engine optimisation, search engine optimizqtion, search engine optimizwtion, search engine optimizztion, search engine optimiza5ion, search engine optimiza6ion, search engine optimizagion, search engine optimizafion, search engine optimizat8on, search engine optimizat9on, search engine optimizatkon, search engine optimizatjon, search engine optimizati9n, search engine optimizati0n, search engine optimizatiln, search engine optimizatikn, search engine optimizatioh, search engine optimizatioj